Math Is Everywhere!
MATH WITH MONEY

By Claire Romaine

Gareth Stevens
PUBLISHING

Please visit our website, www.garethstevens.com. For a free color catalog of all our high-quality books, call toll free 1-800-542-2595 or fax 1-877-542-2596.

Library of Congress Cataloging-in-Publication Data

Names: Romaine, Claire, author.
Title: Math with money / Claire Romaine.
Description: New York : Gareth Stevens Publishing, [2017] | Series: Math is everywhere! | Includes index.
Identifiers: LCCN 2015045883 | ISBN 9781482446241 (pbk.) | ISBN 9781482446180 (library bound) | ISBN 9781482445985 (6 pack)
Subjects: LCSH: Arithmetic–Juvenile literature. | Money–Juvenile literature.
Classification: LCC HG221.5 .R65 2017 | DDC 513–dc23
LC record available at http://lccn.loc.gov/2015045883

First Edition

Published in 2017 by
Gareth Stevens Publishing
111 East 14th Street, Suite 349
New York, NY 10003

Copyright © 2017 Gareth Stevens Publishing

Editor: Therese Shea
Designer: Sarah Liddell

Photo credits: Cover, p. 1 Thomas J. Sebourn/Shutterstock.com; p. 5 (pennies) Claudio Divizia/Shutterstock.com; p. 5 (sidewalk) Marquisphoto/Shutterstock.com; p. 7 (piggy bank) ptnphoto/Shutterstock.com; pp. 7, 9, 24 (nickels) rsooll/Shutterstock.com; p. 9 (piggy bank) 23 Monkey Business Images/Shutterstock.com; pp. 11, 13, 24 (table) Evgeny Karandaev/Shutterstock.com; pp. 11, 13, 24 (dimes) Paul Cullen Photography/Shutterstock.com; pp. 15, 24 (hand) Denys Prykhodov/Shutterstock.com; pp. 15, 17, 24 (quarters) Abel Tumik/Shutterstock.com; p. 17 (hand) Maryna Pleshkun/Shutterstock.com; p. 19 Chris Ryan/OJO Images/Getty Images; p. 21 Lisa F. Young/Shutterstock.com.

Printed in the United States of America

CPSIA compliance information: Batch #CS16GS: For further information contact Gareth Stevens, New York, New York at 1-800-542-2595.

Contents

Pennies 4

Nickels 6

Dimes 10

Quarters 14

Add It Up! 18

Words to Know 24

Index. 24

I found 9 pennies!
That is 9 cents.

One nickel is worth
5 cents.

My brother Matt
has 4 nickels.
That is 20 cents.

One dime is worth 10 cents.

I have 2 dimes.
That is 20 cents.

One quarter is worth
25 cents.

Matt has 2 quarters.
That is 50 cents.

Grandpa helps us add our money. Do we have enough to buy ice cream?

Yes! We buy
ice cream cones.
We get money back.
That is called change.

We buy ice cream
for our friends, too!

Words to Know

dime

nickel

quarter

Index

dime 10, 12
nickel 6, 8

pennies 4
quarter 14, 16